Susan Branch

Gratitude

a book of
INSPIRATIONAL THOUGHTS & QUOTES

new seasons®

We are the
hero of
our own story.

♥ Mary McCarthy

"Courage is doing what you're afraid to do. There is no courage unless you're scared."

 EDDIE RICKENBACKER

"Charm: the quality in others
that makes us more
satisfied with ourselves."

♥ Henri-Frédéric Amiel

Never underestimate the value

of the little moment ♡.

THE BEST
THINGS IN LIFE
AREN'T THINGS.

"FRIENDS ~

They are kind to

each other's HOPES.

They cherish

each other's DREAMS."

♥ Thoreau

"The world is my country,
all mankind are my brethren,
and to do good is my religion."

♥ Thomas Paine

"He that is of a merry heart hath a continual feast."

♥ Proverbs 15:15

"The dandelions and buttercups
gild all the lawn; the drowsy bee
stumbles among the clover tops,
and summer sweetens all to me."

J. R. Lowell

"Just living is not enough," said the butterfly.

"One must have sunshine, freedom, and a little flower."
♥ Hans Christian Andersen

I love everything that's old: old friends,
old times, old manners, old books,
old wines. ♥ Oliver Goldsmith

ALL THE FLOWERS OF ALL THE
TOMORROWS ARE IN THE
SEEDS OF TODAY.

Ah! There is nothing like
Staying home for real comfort.
♥ JANE AUSTEN

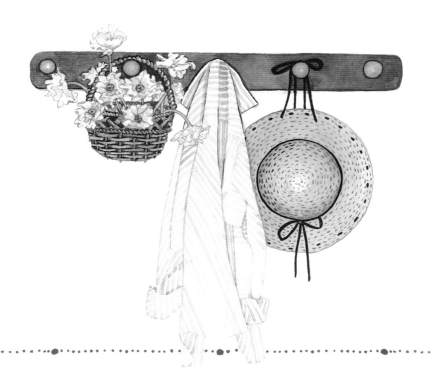

A house is made of walls & beams; a home is built with love & dreams.

 IT IS THE SWEET, SIMPLE THINGS OF LIFE WHICH ARE THE REAL ONES AFTER ALL.  Laura Ingalls Wilder

A SHIP IN HARBOR IS SAFE,

BUT THAT'S NOT WHAT

SHIPS ARE BUILT FOR.

♥ John A. Shedd

" IN COOKING, AS IN ALL
THE ARTS, SIMPLICITY IS
THE SIGN OF PERFECTION."

♥ Curnonsky

To plant
a
seed

is a
hopeful
deed.

"It is perhaps a more fortunate destiny to have a taste for collecting shells than to be born a millionaire."

♥ Robert Louis Stevenson

"Health is the thing
that makes you feel
like now is the best
time of the year."

♥ Franklin Pierce Adams

Everybody likes to find a letter in the mail, but it doesn't happen as often as it used to. Remember, a phone call is nice but a letter is forever. Make someone's day! ♥

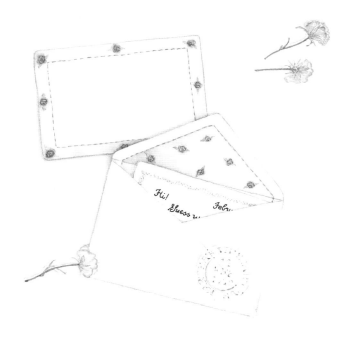

"Manners are a sensitive awareness of the feelings of others. If you have that awareness, you have good manners, no matter what fork you use."

Emily Post ♥

Summer Nights
dark   warm
downtown quiet
    window shop
& eat ice cream

" There's absolutely no reason for being rushed along with the rush. Everybody should be free to go very slow. "

♡ Robt. Frost

YOU ONLY LIVE ONCE
BUT IF YOU WORK IT RIGHT,
ONCE IS ENOUGH.

♥ Mae West

"The simplest pleasures warm true friends most easily." ♥ Alyson Roay

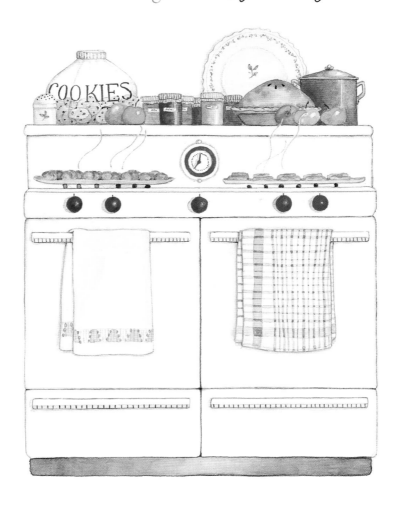

Summer's loss seems little, dear, on days like these. ERNEST DOWSON

Listen! The wind is rising,

and the air is wild with leaves,

We have had our summer evenings,

now for October eves!

Humbert Wolfe

On the road between the
houses of friends
grass does not grow. ♥

The love in your heart
wasn't put there to stay,
love isn't love
till it's
given
away.

"Every man's life is a fairy tale
written by God's fingers."
♥ Hans Christian Andersen

"There is more to life than increasing its speed."

♥ Gandhi

If you were to ask what is most important in a home, I would say memories. — Lillian Gish

EXPLORE.
Dream.
Discover.
Mark Twain

The tide recedes, but leaves behind
bright seashells on the sand.
The sun goes down, but gentle warmth
still lingers on the land.

The music stops, and yet it echoes on in
sweet refrain:

For every joy that passes, something
beautiful remains.

poet unknown

" . . . our life is what our
thoughts make it. "
♥ Marcus Aurelius

Where there is
great love,
There are always
miracles.
♡ Willa Cather

WHEN ONE HAS TASTED WATERMELON

HE KNOWS WHAT THE ANGELS EAT.

♥ Mark Twain

Take
time for
all things.

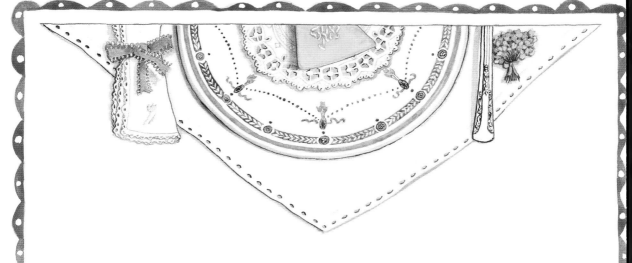

JUST BECAUSE YOU HAVE
FOUR CHAIRS, SIX PLATES,
AND THREE CUPS IS NO REASON
WHY YOU CAN'T INVITE TWELVE
TO DINNER. *Alice May Brock*

"To invite a person
into your house
is to take charge
of his happiness
for as long as he
is under your roof." ♥

A. BRILLAT—SAVARIN

What is the good of your stars and trees, your sunrise and the wind, if they do not enter into our daily lives? E.M. Forster

Great, wide, beautiful, wonderful World,
With the wonderful water round you curled,
And the wonderful grass upon your breast,
World, you are beautifully dressed.
♥ W. B. Rands

" 'Stay' is a charming word
in a friend's vocabulary."
Louisa May Alcott

"Love is friendship set to music."
Anonymous

W**HEN YOU COME
RIGHT DOWN TO
IT, THE SECRET
OF HAVING IT ALL
IS BELIEVING
THAT YOU DO♥.**

No pessimist ever discovered

the secrets of the stars,

or sailed to an uncharted land,

or opened a new heaven

to the human spirit.

Helen Keller

"A good cook is like a sorceress who dispenses happiness." ELSA SCHIAPARELLI ♥

" Thank God for tea! What would the world do without tea? — how did it exist? I am glad I was not born before tea." ♥ Sydney Smith

ONE OF THE
LUCKIEST THINGS
THAT CAN HAPPEN
TO YOU IN LIFE
IS TO HAVE A
HAPPY CHILDHOOD.

Agatha Christie

Family faces are magic mirrors.

Looking at people who belong to us

we see the past, present, & future.

 GAIL LUMET BUCKLEY

"Who bends a knee where violets grow, a hundred secret things shall know."

♥ Rachel Field

ONE OF THE SECRETS OF A HAPPY LIFE IS CONTINUOUS SMALL TREATS. ♥ *Iris Murdoch*

Every act of love

is a work of peace

no matter how small.

❤ Mother Teresa

A loving heart

is the truest wisdom.

♥ CHARLES DICKENS

TRUTH

LITTLE DROPS OF WATER,

LITTLE GRAINS OF SAND,

MAKE THE MIGHTY OCEAN

AND THE PLEASANT LAND.

THUS THE LITTLE MINUTES,

HUMBLE THOUGH THEY BE,

MAKE THE MIGHTY AGES

of eternity.

— Julia A. Fletcher

There are only two ways to live your life. One is as though nothing is a miracle. The other is as if everything is.

ALBERT EINSTEIN

And the song,
from beginning to end,
I found
in the heart of a friend.

HENRY WADSWORTH LONGFELLOW

There are 2 ways

of spreading light —

to be the candle

or the mirror

that reflects it.

♥ Edith Wharton

God respects me when I work,

but He loves me when I sing.

RABINDRANATH TAGORE

Faith is the bird that feels the light and sings when the dawn is still dark. R. Tagore

"EARTH LAUGHS IN FLOWERS."

Ralph Waldo Emerson

"Long live the sun which gives us such color."

♥ Paul Cézanne

IT'S THE LITTLE THINGS
THAT MEAN THE MOST

Winning-the-lottery type happiness is short lived ~ even a trip to Disney World or a new car won't do it for the long term. It's the little things in life: play with your cat, plant a garden, take your kids to the park, bake a pie, take time to be a friend. ♡ Keep putting the little moments together & they'll turn to

CONTENTMENT.

" My little old dog: A heart-beat at my feet."
Edith Wharton

Breathless, we flung us
on the windy hill,
Laughed in the sun,
& kissed the lovely grass.

♥ Rupert Brooke

Happiness grows
at our own firesides
and is <u>not</u> to
be picked in
strangers' gardens.

♥ ♥ ♥

Douglas Jerrold

WITH POMP, POWER & GLORY THE WORLD BECKONS VAINLY,
IN CHASE OF SUCH VANITIES WHY SHOULD I ROAM?

WHILE PEACE & CONTENT BLESS MY LITTLE THATCHED COTTAGE,
AND WARM MY OWN HEARTH WITH THE TREASURES OF HOME.

♥ BEATRIX POTTER

Then I look up through
leafless branches, as I never
can in any other season,
& see the stars shine
in heaven. ANON.

HEARTS CAN
INSPIRE
OTHER HEARTS
WITH THEIR
FIRE.

"All that mankind has done, thought or been: it is in magic preservation, in the pages of books."

— Thomas Carlyle

THE END